FLOOD SONG

FLOOD
SONG

Sherwin Bitsui

Copper Canyon Press
Port Townsend, Washington

Cover art: Sherwin Bitsui, *Drought,* 1999. Oil on canvas,
54 × 44 inches. Photograph by Walter Bigbee. Courtesy of the
Institute of American Indian Arts Museum, Santa Fe.

Copper Canyon Press is in residence at Fort Worden State
Park in Port Townsend, Washington, under the auspices of
Centrum. Centrum is a gathering place for artists and creative
thinkers from around the world, students of all ages and
backgrounds, and audiences seeking extraordinary cultural
enrichment.

LIBRARY OF CONGRESS CATALOGING-IN-PUBLICATION DATA
Bitsui, Sherwin, 1975–
Flood song / Sherwin Bitsui.
    p. cm.
ISBN 978-1-55659-308-6 (pbk.: alk. paper)
1. Navajo Indians—Poetry.   I. Title.
PS3602.I85F56 2009
811'.6—dc22

                                    2009024433

COPPER CANYON PRESS
Post Office Box 271
Port Townsend, Washington 98368
www.coppercanyonpress.org

for my parents, James and Earlene

ACKNOWLEDGMENTS

My deepest gratitude to the Mrs. Giles Whiting Foundation
for their generous support, and to Lannan Foundation for
allowing me time in Marfa, Texas, to begin this body of work.
I would also like to extend my appreciation to the Montana
Artists Refuge and Soul Mountain Retreat.

My grateful acknowledgments to *Narrative, Black Renaissance/
Renaissance Noire, Sou'wester, American Indian* (Smithsonian
National Museum of the American Indian), *Southwestern
American Literature, LIT, Future Earth, To Topos: Ahani,* and
Red Ink, where versions of these poems have appeared.

I wish to also express my appreciation to my family: James
and Earlene, Jolene, Jamie, Lyle, and James Jr. To my extended
family: the Tłizíłaaní of T'iis tsoznaat'í, the Bįįbito'nii
Tódích'ii'nii of Bida'dzígai, and the Ma'iideeshgizhnii of
Tsezhin chxǫ'í, Arizona, and also to Sonja Kravanja, Arthur
Sze, Michael Wiegers, Allison Hedge Coke, S.G. Frazier,
Orlando White, Phil Hall, Jonn Davis, Gabriel Lopez Shaw,
and Valaurie Yazzie—without their support and friendship
this book would not have been possible.

Ná ho kos, ná ho kos, ná ho kos

REX LEE JIM

FLOOD SONG

tó

tó

tó

tó

tó

tó

tó

I bite my eyes shut between these songs.

They are the sounds of blackened insect husks
                                    folded over elk teeth in a tin can,

they are gull wings fattening on cold air
                    flapping in a paper sack on the chlorine-stained floor.

They curl in corners, spiked and black-thatched,
stomp across the living-room ceiling,
pull our hair one strand at a time from electric sockets
and paint our stems with sand in the kitchen sink.

They speak a double helix,
zigzag a tree trunk,
bark the tips of its leaves with cracked amber—

        they plant whispers where shouts incinerate into hisses.

Stepping through the drum's vibration,
I hear gasoline
        trickle alongside the fenced-in panorama
of the reed we climb in from
and slide my hands into shoes of ocean water.

I step onto the gravel path of swans paved across lake scent,
wrap this blank page around the exclamation point slammed between us.

The storm lying outside its fetal shell
folds back its antelope ears
and hears its heart pounding through powdery earth
underneath dancers flecking dust from their ankles to thunder into rain.

I am unable to pry my fingers from the ax,
        unable to utter a word
                without Grandfather's accent rippling
around the stone flung into his thinning mattress.

Years before, he would have named this season
        by flattening a field where grasshoppers jumped into black smoke.

A crow snaps beak over and over again:
the past is a blurry splotch of red crosshatched with neon light;
     on the drive south,
            windows pushed down,
        you scoop pellets of canned air
   and ocean across sand dunes,
       across the waning lick of moonlight on the dashboard
       to crease the horizon
          between petals of carved snow.

Bluebirds chirp icy rocks from their stomachs
and crash,
      wings caked heavy
with the dark mud of a gunmetal sky,
to the earth's bandages
      shivering with cold spells and convulsions
         in the market
            underneath an avalanche of apples.

A redtail hawk scrapes the sandstone wall with its beak.

A shower of sparks skate across the morning sky.

You think this bottle will open a canyon wall
      and light a trail
           trampled by gloved hands
as you inhale earth, wind, water,
through the gasoline nozzle
     at trail's end,
          a flint spear driven into the key switch.

You think you can return to that place
where your mother held her sleeves above the rising tides
saying, "We are here again
         on the road covered with television snow;
            we are here again
               the song has thudded."

Bison horns twist into the sides of trains
    winding through the broth-filled eyes of hens
        squawking from the icebox;

shock-coils from the jet engine's roar
        erupt from the memory of splintered eagle-wing bone.

Pinned down with icicles on the loosening floor,
        an alarm clock wails from speaker box to speaker box
            probing for hornet nests inside the tourmaline seeds of dawn;

its scalp *scalpeled* alongside what is "ours";
        its memory of bone axes x-ed out with chrome engine paint.

Flicking off the light switch.
Lichen buds the curved creases of a mind
pondering the mesquite tree's dull ache
      as it gathers its leaves around clouds of spotted doves—
          calling them in rows of twelve back from their winter sleep.

Doves' eyes black as nightfall
shiver on the foam coast of an arctic dream
      where whale ribs
          clasp and fasten you to a language of shifting ice.

Seeing into those eyes
you uncoil their telephone wires,
gather their inaudible lions with plastic forks,
tongue their salty ribbons,
      and untie their weedy stems from your prickly fingers.

You stop to wonder what *like* sounds like
when held under glacier water,
how *Ná ho kos* feels
under the weight of all that loss.

I cover my eyes with electrical wires,
see yellow dawn eclipse Stop signs,
        turn green and screech into phosphorescence.

Each flickering finger:
a memory of a flashing yellow sign,
blinks between charcoal sheets of monsoon rain
then slices through the thawing of our hunger
with the cracked eaves of a shattered house.

Its autobiographical muscle—
stringing trees into a forest, convulses,
only to be flattened under its metallic leaves
and sold as bricks for its basement of fire.

What land have you cast from the blotted-out region of your face?

What nation stung by watermarks was filmed out of extinction and brought forth resembling frost?

What offspring must jump through the eye of birth to be winked at when covered with brick sweat?

What ache piled its planks on the corner pier, now crumbles onto motionless water, sniffed at by forest smoke?

What makes this song a string of beads seized by cement cracks when the camera climbs through the basement window—winter clouds coiling through its speckled lens?

What season cannot locate an eye in the dark of the sound of the sun gyrating into red ocher after I thought you noticed my language was half wren, half pigeon and, together, we spoke a wing pattern on the wall that was raised to keep "us" out, there where "calling" became "culling," "distance" distanced, in a mere scrape of enamel on yellow teeth?

What father woke, turned over his wife, she didn't want to, but he pushed until the baby leapt through, now, now, now, strummed into a chorus of burn marks on ceilings where police sirens fruit magpie skulls on trees of monsoon lightning?

What, what, what—is how the song chimed in wilderness.

Pinched from sunlight's jagged leaf,
the singer's skin
a fingerprint on muddy river water
        crowns our whispers with sharp talons.

His shrill cry—
scraped down to a thumbnail with television knobs—
        becomes the wailing that returns to the Reservation.

You follow him across sand dunes,
warm his hand with your breath
and place inside the buckskin satchel:
                harp strings of reassembled moonlight,
                thumbprints of ocean water,
                and a key to the back door of a burning church.

He sponges the deck of their leaking boat invisible
       on the horizon spilling its name on rusted knives
           to make it stop, sigh, then whisper *sleep*
           to animals kicking loose the oven's door.

The tick of the clock blotted the exit from the mind
hours before the ravens could swirl into this new instinct,
this new hue—
pressing open the wound,
       a field of gnats foaming from its half smile.

I strike a wet match on his wooden mind,
stash my invitation behind his waterless eyes,
and pencil in the first unmarked box:

Dark matter in the blue scarf,
        crumpled map, smashed compass,
                back there—I can feel the faces of wolves.

His music fermented
the cheek of a songbird inscribed on doe meat,
and handed the oven its first match
before he collapsed on his one new idea
circled by tears underwater where a buoy—
strapped to a glass plow—
        cradled the farmer's pitchfork and scythe.

Obsidian blades in here—he said,
"You will count two in the silences between the gaps of our bodies;
three in the fibrous matter of our crossing;
four in the nurse's gown as she reaches in;
five in the rough cage of our silence:
cylindrical in the mind
      that wants to *chameleon* from the gray that crowds in."

Breath, steam,
    who could tell the difference.

An ax in his hand,
he heard a crow digging wren eggs
from beaks tied with eyelash hair
and asked the summer,
"What happened in the ellipses?
What happened when gunfire blew into their speech
and left one language hanging by a nail
at the entrance of mouths
flooded with such things as the down of drowned herons
and the mud-covered hooves of drought
kicking at the rain-stained earth
devoured by minutes and seconds
sticking to their shoes like sap,
their onions peeled back,
bees dangling like half moths out of their eyes?"

He wanted to hold back gas-soaked doves with a questioning glance;
he wanted the clock to tick downwind from this gavel and pew,
from this leash, bucket, drainpipe, and mildewed cracker,
from the mind's muddy swan served on a platter with lemon rinds,
from spiders scurrying over its bone-polished surface,
from crosshatches punched into its shredded time card,
from the desert near the tree line where the molting must have begun,
where crushed bodies heave warm, jellylike,
in the thicket at the foot of the wandering,
perched inside their velveteen shirts,
chirping crimson, then vermilion, then rust,
as the water's song wilts the petals of splayed bullets
spilling from ceramic pots into stovepipes,
as the yelping of lambs rutted with wagon tracks
bubbles from glass tubes, triangular in their circular sleep patterns.

Hummingbirds scratch out the last tooth
from the doorknob held up as an offering to the sun.

Horses gallop toward the hive in which our fingers claw the slit:

computer light trickles in from under moist fingernails;

a twig yanked from the nervous eye of a dying bull
grows from red earth,
becomes the oar we use to sop aside our thirst;

they want you to speak open a window slick with Coyote's sweat
trail poems onto ladders of forest smoke
      and hoist into bed
with the bristles of the broom you write *freedom* with
      a blanket of questions billowing like windswept feathers out of our closed eyes

until there is no tongue to smooth away the hairline fracture between *us* and *them.*

In a stadium of afterglow—
        I parcel ounces of my body for each acre grazed,
        spear my hands with my sharpened knees
                to keep some kernel of this trail my own,
        some piece of the idea of *now*
            before it becomes *was.*

Chipped along the scalloped edges of flint,
this captive house opens its windows
as you dream green
        the antelope growling from the inner ring
                of the pictograph's central spiral.

You notice,
leaning inside the broom closet:
a fur mop peyote-stitched to the wet floor;
star maps—dappled with frost—
lifted with the gavel when a highway begins swerving
        out of the rain-drenched kitchen.

It is here that they scoop granite stones from your chest,
snap each rib shut over the highway leading south,

comb your hair over pine smoke—
dreaming out of the ship that carried their shackles here.

Their blue squeal—rectilinear in predawn air—
blows northward followed by a fog of galloping horses.

It is here they shake down branches to lift the veil
        so the water of our clans may keep from gushing out—

and leave in its muddied path:
strips of grief swelling luminous between the chest, its plate bone
        and the dimming atlases of our lungs.

There is no sign of the trail leading out,
only a pond of mule blood at the basin of the dam
resting between us.

Together we climb the song's hair,
step onto the plank
and hear birth cries erupt into a bridge of starlight
connecting the ink-soaked shores of our nameless bodies
to anchors of swans
        coughing dune sand onto a dry riverbed.

Lifting the cloth to smear the reed invisible,
I notice spiders emerging where our hair slipped out
and leap by firelight
into the raft scribbled on pond water,
        its translucent oars chiming metallic as it sinks below sea level.

The aching inserted sideways underneath the linoleum floor
begins to sound less like weeping,
and more like the cawing of crows,
gathering,
        thirsty, fat bellied,
            outside the keyhole,
for whom we have become bodies for the first time,
    for whom our language stabs the fork with a spoon.

I carve this apple into a dove,
wrap it in a nest of boiling water.

I pinch your silences into soft whispers,
pile them on your still chest—
        the marrows of turtles swirling counterclockwise inside them.

I offer a dry stem,
        unfold this paper crane into a square cage.

I keep the butcher's thumbprints here.

I scratch flat earth with the balls of my feet,
hear a scythe chiming inside the hairline crack of a canyon wall,
and dig asphalt from the obsidian mouth of the carved horse,
its knotted mane chain-linked to a past—

                                       gray as the sting of sleep.
My coal-dusted boots hammered into its turquoise glance.

Those who congregated
to heat the room
swore to never do it   again,
      never whip the mare,
      feed it bee stings,
or dice fishing line and bait
      horizontally on the mattress
          to be mauled by wolves
          that leave paw prints over our tangled hair.

Downwind from the body's yellow teeth,
children whisper *night*—
    amniotic clouds of car exhaust
        foaming to a lather above them.

They are later found deboned—
plucked from the narrowing field—
ears pulled back,
    a nation growling into them
    as they scrape double-plumed birdsongs
        from the beaks of drowned hummingbirds
    and smash them into eagle-bone whistles
        then ringlets of fire
            then the blood of orphaned lambs.

Sifting atlas blue from yellow body   here again,

gaveling the nail of the first ship   here again,

crating star maps in corn husk   here again,

unfurling a blank heaven over mapped earth   here again,

the time to leave   here again,

to turn bone white   here again,

an elk's shadow rising behind us   here again.

Near the Stop sign
on the trailhead beside the plot

the final chapter of this one-room story
smells disfigured

before I wince
at its cigarette-burned couch.

I compare my hands to what I imagine thought might look like
when suspended in fossilized amber,

release the captured mosquito from my closed hands,
string dimming gas lamps between rain and fall,

and insert into the knife's pale origin—
        a twig warming the clutching hand.

This windowless house marrows my veins with thinking.

Scraps of venison leaf the picture frame.

A stoplight dangles from the sunbeam of a birth song
billowing from stratus
      to cumulus
           to nimbus
               to drought,

as the ache of ten cedar trees silences the dull ax.

You should have seen
       the shrew
torn to
       tendon, snout, fur, claw

by the mountain stream
          under bright moonlight,

small as a baby's fist—
          it spiraled in the crashing waves.

The luminous wander cornfields without husbands;
their wooden faces splinter the owl's nest;

their tongues scraped bone smooth with cartilage,
speak the gray language of black stones.

They throb in the cornfield.
They quake out of silence bleating across engine growl.

They will trail us.
They will wake with eagle whistles in their mouths.

We drill crumbs of ewe hair into the door hinge:

yellow dust blankets withers steaming in dog sweat;

red ants weave mud mandibles into nostrils
hushed by boot heels pounding flat
every inch of sand between our daughters and sons;

the horse's hooves smash hospital gurneys
into spokes of blue static
blinking clear:

    the son carved from the driver's seat

        his hand on the wheel

           his hair reaching for spring water.

A whip's leather scent flails camera shutters
open to the softened teeth of masked dancers—

their salty sweat swells loose bone stirrups
tethering our feet to coils of lightning
wafting from under a mane of winter clouds.

Pressing a handful of chipped house paint
against their smeared faces,
you say,
"We need this color of wing's blood
in the dark of our bodies crouching away from thirst,"
then pluck with a dull knife:
teeth from rocks gnawing
into the memory of the belt's hiss
shoved *here* and *there,*
       squabbling through the wall
            stretching out between us.

They lather lung milk over the television's white backdrop,
push blackened wicks into the whites of their mothers' downcast eyes.

The width of their hue
itching through weathered boot soles
blackens their snared breath with coal dust.

Their wood-grain hands cascading west—
        sharp and final as the train tracks
                upon which we cut loose these saddles.

With a gaping mouth,
I sought an image to describe the knot in my chest,
the car door jammed—

     the land divided into two new car scents.

Coyote howls canyons into windows painted on the floor with crushed turquoise;

captured cranes secrete radon in the *epoxied* toolshed;

leopard spots, ripe for drilling, ooze white gas when hung on a copper wire.

I pull electricity from their softened bellies with loom yarn.

I map a shrinking map.

We row toward the oar wet with deer blood
and onward to the edge that must be crossed
with crosses hammered into it.

I see their footprints in fresh snow.

The soft spot of their childhood heads
pushed branchless into the parched earth.

Gray amnesia swirling after songbirds in its dome.

The distance they traveled
chipped down to a few powdery beginnings
in the arroyo with flies buzzing out of it.

I hear the crackle of sawdust sliding down our throats.

I notice there is no fur left for the ghosts of mammals.

Gnawing coarse hair from
       the ink-splattered eaves of the darkened house
              they attempt to pull the survivor from its flood
but stop to comment on how dark his skin is
       how wooden his face looks
              when photographed on a horse facing west;

as if to name reeds piercing the horse's neck: *whale bones wrapped in turtle hide,*

as if to reach into the loom's ribs and wring bear blood from handspun red wool.

You trace deboned wings of ospreys with hawk talons
in the grocery line where the Navajo name for Pleiades is pinched and shredded,
and we dart away thinking: *This is escape, it'll be over soon,*
we have never bothered to grieve, over... soon...

Piling mesquite racks inside the memory of the oar
you watch the boat fizzle and flake
because snowmelt has risen cracks like lightning scrawl
up to wind and mountain to peak above
our hands unearthing the last season with the cackle of crows.

Hot wind bends juniper limbs over plow and chicken wire.
Rain scent peeled from the wetness of our tongues
moistens the wing tips of birds baking inside a steel wire nest.

We shuffle floor tiles into storm designs,
stack them upright in a kneeling man's prayer,
       and watch hills crumble under the weight of our handprints.

Alarm clocks, eagle plumes,
a moth's unblinking eye
hover from left to right,
in the shrinking room
where the children huddle
        nibbling orange crusts
        from diesel-soaked butterfly wings.

Their dimmed faces—hollowed-out with spoons—
are then folded over lightbulbs
and placed diagonally alongside the freeway
to fill the ear with the clacking of lab mice
swirling toward final light
        in rain buckets shipwrecked
                        on turtle shells near the turnpike.

The meeting hall of their bodies
        piled on lawns
        caked with dying birds cooing at them
                remains landlocked inside the naming of:
                        them, those, not like us...

Black ants drift through the throats of wounded stags;

they scuttle the dictionary's blank page for mention of him without her.

You interject:

This man's hand not my own,

not the tick of the clock that flowered the fence's instinct,

not her hands weaving our hair back from the basket's cracked rim.

In a cornfield at the bottom of a sandstone canyon,
wearing the gloves of this song tightly over closed ears;
the bursting sun presses licks of flame
into our throats swelling with ghost dogs
nibbling on hands that roped off our footprints
keeping what is outside ours tucked
beneath the warmth of their feet cooling to zero,
as they swarm luminous landmines like gnats,
as thunder shakes white sand from wet hair,
as police sirens trickle from water jars onto squash blossoms,
as starlight, opened inside a darkened room,
begins to tell its story from end to beginning   again.

I sensed the knife in your past,
its sharp edge shanked from the canyon stream—
a silver trickle between the book jacket,
nihízaad peeled open inside a diabetic mouth.

The waters of my clans
flash-flooded—
I fell from the white of its eyes—
our fathers had no children to name their own,
no baby's cry to place between argument and arguments.

The commercial flashed a blue path
across the lakes of our veins,
the bluest glint, a rock in the ear
told our tongues entwined

that I was reaching for the cornfield inside you,
that I was longing to outlive this compass
pointing toward my skull
gauzed inside this long terrible whisper

damp in a desert canyon,
whitewashed by the ache of fog lights
reaching to unravel   my combed hair.

Scraping rough with smooth,
      the mind *pillboxes* the scent of a cactus wren
           and wraps it with strands of neon vapor.

Dinetah—scratched out
from the eye with juniper bark—
hunches with engine sweat
curling out of its collar,
its owner—a leash without a hand—
bleeds gasoline
      when lathered with a blur of red bricks.

The song spilling seeds into your mouth
sunflowers a Yield sign,
crawls onto the roof pinching cornmeal,
flickers green
          and quakes into a babble of crows.

It then speaks *splintering* from a polished clay bowl,
drifts onto the lake's shore—
          apostrophes attached to its hemline.

Obsidian slides over the starling's nest
          backhoes nearing the coal shed sputter awake,
a pebble splinters the tribe into half brothers;

                    the pass shrinks to a black dot behind us.

Niłchi
is wind breath
the wave of stars
pulled into a satchel
scattered on the lake's slate surface.

Our sour scent pulses outward from the birth sac's metallic fumes.

Our palms sail to the first drop of cold water,
after sinking an anvil into the belly's thirst.

Waiting with the gate key
we devour any mention of returning with sacks of sea salt
and untwist this flood's doorknobs with transparent hands;

we enter the village unfolding screeches.

They inherit a packet of earth
hear its coins clank in a tin box

push *them* aside
reap thick strands of night from thinning black hair.

They climb the staircase clenching branches of pens filled with ducks' blood

and follow the butcher's bed into this room—
       goose feathers thorning out of their eyes.

They promise to never look down again
down is just a speck of globe dust

                just coins clanking in the tin box.

Heat waves lift our fingers from the mud-smeared windshield;

a wren, shredded by the beaks of black birds, spins in the grip of its slipstream;

a wet rat flopping on the bear's stretched hide
      shakes through a needle's eye in its own stanza of white light;

a horse, stung by bees, bucks inside the singer's mind
        as he spills night from his rattle,
like shaking the last minutes of prayer
      from your mouth at the gas station.

Landlocked in the debris of a broken drum,
stirred with turtle bones,
a zigzag flashes out of the deer's nostrils:
its ribs silhouetted against starlight,

its song—canopied and threaded with fishing line—
is again scraped from the driest month with rabbitbrush,

as if the footprints actually led here,
as if our tracks bled from the snouts of wounded bison,

as if we wanted this cloth lifted,
these stones hurled out, this chasm stitched shut.

I retrace and trace over my fingerprints.
Here: magma,
there: shore,

and on the peninsula of his finger pointing west—
a bell rope woven from optic nerves
       is tethered to mustangs galloping from a nation lifting its first page
            through the manhole—burn marks in the saddle horn,
                  static in the ear that cannot sever cries from wailing.

                  I did not blink shut

I could have hatched the egg
of the imagined Reservation
and not fear the quickening of my blood
       or *theirs* pounding upright
            in the money vault.

I walk my hair's length over tire ruts,
crush seedpods with thumbnails,
push kernels of corn
into dove nests on the gnarled branches of our drowned lungs.

Mining saguaro pulp from garden rock,
squeezing coarse black hair—
I arrive at a map of a face buried in spring snow.

With a plastic cup
I scrape the enamel chips of morning songs
        from the kitchen sink,
and breathe through my eyelids,
glimpsing the thawing of our flat world.

I dial into the blue skin of the map's stiff pulse,
emeralds spill from the skull's cavernous wail,
but nightfall is still darkest
in the middle stanza of the poem
          arching twenty miles past forgiveness.

The poem
          held out to the wind
          speaks *juniper* to the wilderness,
as August slithers into September's copper pipes
searching for the paw print of a waterfall
                    on the mind's lunar surface.

Here—I thread nightfall into the roan's black mane.
Here—I peel a paper mask from the hare's moist cartilage.
Here—tornadoes twist into the loom's black yarn,
but the premonition—
beginning with three masts and a cross—
still mushrooms over the groans of husbands and wives
folding their petals outward
from their salt-coated bodies
          saying... *nihi yazhi, nihaaneendza,*
                    nihi yazhi, niha aneendza.

          our child, you have returned to us,
                    our child you have returned to us.

I wanted to swallow the song's flowers, swim diagonally its arched back, its shadow stinging my hands with black pollen.

We were on the same surgical table waiting for the surgeons to carve us back into shape.

The drum pulsed somewhere in the dark and I heard a woman unbraiding her hair.

I felt morning songs leap from the *hooghan*'s smoke-hole and curl outward from the roof of the sky, gliding through us like rain.

I sang, sang until the sun rose.

The shadows of my face grew into a swallow with folded wings and darted into the fire.

A cloud became a skull and crashed to the earth above Black Mesa.

The cloud wanted to slip through the coal mines and unleash its horses.

It wanted to crack open bulldozers and spray their yolk over the hills so that a new birth cry would awaken the people who had fallen asleep.

It wanted to push their asymmetrical ramblings into the weft of storm blanket, dye it hazel and sink it into the rising waters.

A city dragged its bridges behind it and finally collapsed in a supermarket asking for the first apple that was ever bitten.

No one questioned the sand anymore.

No one untucked themselves from their bodies and wandered the streets without knowing their clans.

Everyone planted corn in their bellies and became sunlight washing down plateaus with deer running out of them.

The phone was ringing through it all.

The line was busy when I picked the ax
     and chose the first tree   to chop down.

ABOUT THE AUTHOR

Sherwin Bitsui is originally from White Cone, Arizona, on the Navajo Reservation. He is Diné of the Tódích'ii'nii (Bitter Water Clan), born for the Tłizíłaaní (Many Goats Clan). He holds an A.F.A. from the Institute of American Indian Arts Creative Writing Program and is currently completing his studies at the University of Arizona in Tucson. He also works for literacy programs that bring poets and writers into public schools where there are Native American student populations. Bitsui has published his poems in *American Poet, The Iowa Review, Frank* (Paris), *LIT,* and elsewhere. His poems were also anthologized in *Legitimate Dangers: American Poets of the New Century.*

The Chinese character for poetry is made up of two parts: "word" and "temple." It also serves as pressmark for Copper Canyon Press.

Since 1972, Copper Canyon Press has fostered the work of emerging, established, and world-renowned poets for an expanding audience. The Press thrives with the generous patronage of readers, writers, booksellers, librarians, teachers, students, and funders—everyone who shares the belief that poetry is vital to language and living.

Major funding has been provided by:

Amazon.com

Anonymous

Beroz Ferrell & The Point, LLC

Cynthia Hartwig and Tom Booster

Golden Lasso, LLC

Lannan Foundation

National Endowment for the Arts

Cynthia Lovelace Sears and Frank Buxton

Washington State Arts Commission

For information and catalogs:

COPPER CANYON PRESS
Post Office Box 271
Port Townsend, Washington 98368
360-385-4925
www.coppercanyonpress.org

This book is set in Parable, designed for digital composition by Christopher Burke in 2002. Book design and composition by Valerie Brewster, Scribe Typography. Printed on archival-quality paper at McNaughton & Gunn, Inc.

Printed in the USA
CPSIA information can be obtained
at www.ICGtesting.com
JSHW052019140824
68134JS00027B/2553